THE CHILDREN

AT

THE PHALANSTERY.

THE CHILDREN

AT

THE PHALANSTERY.

A FAMILIAR DIALOGUE ON EDUCATION.

BY F. CANTAGREL.

TRANSLATED BY
FRANCIS GEO. SHAW.

BOSTON:
WILLIAM D. TICKNOR & CO.

1848.

R. CRAIGHEAD, PRINTER & STEREOTYPER,
112 FULTON STREET.

PREFACE.

THERE are few households in which the children are not heard crying from morning till night: the mother-in-law says it is the fault of her daughter-in-law; the parents and friends, that it is the fault of the child; uninterested persons make the consoling reflection, that in a more advanced age more serious causes of sorrow will incessantly be found. In the meanwhile the mother and the child console each other by a tender embrace; joy and smiles reappear upon all faces. A few moments afterwards, fresh tears—

Whom must we decide to be right, and whom wrong? We must first decide that the children are right, and then that the grown persons are wrong. Who pretend to be reasonable? The grown persons certainly; and there they are about the children, worrying, fussing, without being able to divine the cause of those tears; still more, they themselves very often cause those innocent tears to flow, by their ignorance, their harshness, their fancies; they pretend to regulate at their will the tastes of those children, and their steps, their words and their gestures.

But no, we must not yet blame the parents and the friends; alas! they do what they can, they do what they have been taught, and it is not their fault if they do not succeed any better. We must blame all those philosophers, all those august doctors, who pretend to govern all things, and who know nothing; they think they have penetrated the secrets of nature, and during the ages that great and small have lived in tears, they have not known how to dry a single one; and, very often, their false wisdom has mingled blood with the tears of the poor human race.

Oh! their pride may take offence! "Do we pay any attention to those little monkeys?" they will haughtily reply; "such cares are unworthy of us, we do not stoop to such low details."

And you do well; the least intelligent mother knows more on that point than all your presumptuous systems; but your fault, your inexcusable fault, is in extolling a social order so false, so badly constructed, that the best desires of the mother cannot succeed in any manner, the best instincts of the child cannot be brought forth, and everything goes every moment in opposition to nature and the divine laws.

All things are bound together in nature, and if your social order engenders evil and infinite suffering for men and for women of all ranks and all conditions, it is a very simple thing that it should produce a result quite as disastrous in the case of children. And look at those children—I do not even speak of poor children, I speak only of rich children, or those in comfortable circumstances; see those little things, imprisoned, constrained, tortured in their instinctive movements. Is there but one in a family? he is overwhelmed with murderous caresses, with idolatrous and destructive attentions; constantly deprived of the sight, of the company of other children, he has around him, only smiling faces, it may be—but those smiles are often not young enough to satisfy him. Is there any spectacle more affecting than that which chance sometimes presents to us, that of a young child who can see, touch, embrace, another child of its own age? there is a moment of happiness which is worth more to him than all the caresses of his parents, excepting those of his mother.

If, on the contrary, there are several brothers and sisters in the same family, the difference in tastes and characters, and very often the unjust preferences of parents, excite incessant quarrels and interminable bickerings.

Must these children be separated then? No; but they must have a greater liberty, that is, they must be placed in a more numerous infantile assemblage, where they can be developed more freely, and choose their companions according to the agreements or the contrasts of their characters.

Too restricted relations of the child in the narrow circle of his parents, or of his brothers and sisters, and the consequent compression, stifling of his instincts—this is the shoal on which the education of early childhood incessantly strikes, or is wrecked, without this fact having been as yet understood.

The following dialogue contains the development of this idea, applied to the education of early childhood, and consequently to that of youth.

It is extracted from a work published in 1841, by M. F. Cantagrel, under the title of " Le Fou du Palais-Royal," in which the author has stated, under the varied form of a dialogue, the most important points of the societary Theory of Fourier.

Some of the words used by the author being either new, or employed in a special sense, it is necessary to give some definitions.

The reader may know that Fourier has stated scientifically the law of the conditions according to which the association of men among themselves must be established: it is the aggregate of Fourier's views that we call the *societary Theory*.

In going over the history of the past, Fourier discerned in the different situations in which humanity has found itself placed by turns, certain phases which it was easy to distinguish by particular traits: these are, Savageism, Patriarchalism and Barbarism. There is, moreover, a fourth period, to which Europe, particularly, has attained in our day: this is *Civilization*.

In the writings of Fourier, and in the following dialogue, this word Civilization is not therefore, most frequently, used in its customary signification, which vaguely indicates the general state of the intellectual and moral culture of a people; it has a more restricted, and more precise meaning; it indicates only a special period, one of the stations in the advance of Humanity.

In the same manner as Fourier had distinguished several successive periods in the past, so he foresaw them in the future: the most advanced of all, the most beautiful, the most rich, the most happy, he calls *Harmony*, wishing to indicate thereby the agreement which will then exist among all the inhabitants of the globe, and their obedience to the laws of the Creator. *Harmonian*, means the man of the ages of *Harmony*.

Every day, in our present society, we designate by the words, *savage, barbarian*, the men who live, or have lived, in the periods of savageism and of barbarism, evidently inferior to the period of *civilization*. Let no one be shocked therefore, we entreat, if we sometimes apply, with a slight shade of disdain, the name *civilizes* to the men living in *civilization;* the reason is, that we foresee periods superior to that *civilization;* and, most certainly, our descendants, when they shall have escaped from the gulf of miseries, of cheatery, and of desolation, in which we struggle, will speak of the *civilizees* with much more commiseration than we now do of the barbarians and savages.

The *Phalanstery* is the unitary building in which dwell the population of the associated township, and, by extension, we give the name of *Phalanstery* to the whole of the buildings, the territory, the cultivation, the labors, and the general course of activity of that *associated township*, which is the antipodes of the divided, *parcelled* township, such as it exists now.

The *Phalanx* is the aggregate of the population which inhabits the associated township.

We call the inhabitant of the phalanstery, *Phalansterian*, as we call the inhabitant of a city, *citizen*, and of a village, *villager*.

There being no phalansteries as yet, the name of *Phalansterians* is also given, and we accept this qualification provisorily, to those who, after having studied and understood the social science discovered by Fourier, believe and hope that the earth will one day be covered with phalansteries, in which shall reign peace, riches, happiness, and the religious harmony of created beings with their kind and with the Creator, and who, by their labors, endeavor to hasten the epoch of this advent of Humanity to its true destiny.

These explanations appear to us sufficient to enable the following pages to be read without difficulty. We recommend them to the attention of all mothers of families.

THE CHILDREN AT THE PHALANSTERY.

PERSONAGES.

THE MOTHER.
TWO LITTLE CHILDREN.
THE HUSBAND.
X., THE PHALANSTERIAN.
MYSELF, FRIEND OF X.: it is MYSELF who gives an account
of the Dialogue.

I.

THE door opens, and we see the master of the house, who receives us cordially, but not without an excuse for the cries of his youngest, which resound through the apartment.

"My friend," said our host, "I know that you like children; I suppose that this gentleman does not hate them; have the goodness, therefore, to stop your ears, and permit me, gentlemen, to present you to my wife. You have neglected us horribly of late, my dear fellow; my wife complains of it."

X. "She is too good, really; but why do I never meet you?"

"Ah! my friend, when one has children to bring up—"

X. "Yes, yes, I understand."

We were introduced into an apartment in which there were already seven persons; two young children playing upon the carpet, one still younger, crying upon the lap of his mother, around whom three other women, the nurse, the chambermaid and the cook, were making useless attempts to pacify the poor child.

After the usual compliments, seats were offered to us.

"You see," said X. to me in a low voice, taking a seat by my side, "you see here one of the thousand instances of wrong social combinations. Four women after one child! It is sad!"

"What do you say?" asked the husband.

X. "I say, my friend, that with all your happiness you are very unhappy; I say that if you have the delights of paternity you have also its inconveniences, and I add, that this child suffers as much from them as you do."

THE MOTHER. "Oh! sir, the cares which a child requires have also their charm."

X. "I assent to that, madam; but confess that those cares would have a still greater charm, if they were not accompanied by anxieties."

THE HUSBAND. "That is true; but what's to be done?"

X. "Ah! what's to be done? we must"——

THE HUSBAND. "I understand; we must build a Phalanstery."

X. "Certainly; for there you would experience a happiness without alloy in watching over and bringing up your child; and, on his side, the little fellow would be much more happy in the *Seristeries,* and would not wear himself out by crying as he does, to the great detriment of his organs and his health."

THE HUSBAND. "The worst of the matter is, that we cannot find the cause of these cries."

X. "No doubt. In the Seristeries it would be discovered at once."

The child seemed to testify his approval of this view by still more piercing screams.

THE HUSBAND. "What do you mean by *Seristery?*"

X. "Fourier gives the name of Seristery, in general, to the place appropriated to the labors of a Series or industrial corporation; the common atelier of a Series. At the Phalanstery, this noisy little fellow would be very quiet and very comfortable, among children of his own age, in the Seristery of infants."

THE MOTHER (*eagerly*). "Ah! sir, I should not wish to be separated from my son."

X. "Permit me to believe, madam, that if you were certain your son would be more favorably brought up elsewhere than with you, and by others than yourself, you would find strength enough to separate yourself from him; for you love him for his sake, doubtless, and not for yourself. But, madam, it is not even asked that you should lose him from your sight; you are allowed to see him every moment, and even to carry him to your chamber, if you so desire. But you would take good care not to do this if you saw it was injurious to the well-being of the child. At the Phalanstery, all the establishments, all the lodgings, have the advantage of communicating with each other by the street gallery, a principal artery which circulates through the whole edifice and carries movement and life from the centre to the extremities, as do the arteries in the human body. Although he may be in the Seristeries, your child is therefore in fact under your own roof, and yet you avoid the disagreeableness, the inconveniences of a home education."

THE MOTHER. " And if I have a taste for educational labors ?"

X. " Then you will attend to the education of your own child at the same time with that of others, supposing you desire this; but, in any event, you will experience neither the torments nor the anxieties of maternity."

THE MOTHER. "That would be a very beautiful result; but in order to appreciate it, I must know the arrangements of your Phalansteries."

X. " Really, madam, if I were not afraid of being taken for a pedant, I would offer to give you a sketch of them."

THE MOTHER. "How so, sir! on the contrary—An establishment in which you say that children would be so happy, so well brought up! I should like to have an idea of it. Besides, the little my husband has told me has given me a desire to know more. I know that you wish to render labor attractive, and that you pretend to make everybody happy, from the old man to the infant. God grant it may be possible! " My poor little one !" added she, affectionately embracing her child, who redoubled his cries. " Here, Josephine," said she to the nurse, " take him away and try to put him to sleep—it is about the hour—I listen to you, sir."

X. " Really, madam, I hardly know where to begin."

THE HUSBAND. " Oh! you can go on without fear. We are already somewhat informed."

X. " The Phalanstery, or habitation of the Phalanx, is no other than a conveniently and comfortably arranged palace which we substitute for the houses, cottages and huts that now compose our villages.   Now, the Phalanx being a union of about four hundred families or eighteen hundred individuals unequal in age, inclination, fortune, &c., voluntarily associated according to the three productive faculties (*capital, labor and talent*), for all the labors of cultivation, manufacturing, housekeeping, education, &c., it is absolutely necessary that the Phalanstery should conform in its arrangements to the different industrial aptitudes, to the different sensitive, animatic and intellectual wants, to the different passional requirements which will be manifested in the bosom of such an association.   In a word, the distribution of the societary palace must be appropriate to the different orders of those aptitudes, of those wants, of those requirements.   Consequently, in order to state in proper terms the programme of the Phalanstery, we must first know what facts will take place there, what tendencies will be developed ; it is, therefore, necessary to have a profound knowledge of the social science."

THE HUSBAND. " Pass over that."

X. " Yes, I neglect these generalities in order to arrive at the description you desire.   Represent to yourself, therefore, a vast edifice divided into wings, with interior courts and galleries of communication, open in summer, closed and warmed in winter. First imagine two great divisions : one for the noisy workshops, gathered in one of the wings ; the other for the quiet labors, distributed throughout the rest of the edifice, taking into account the passional, industrial and social requirements to which I have referred.   Now suppose that in the centre are the great halls of meeting for the whole Phalanx, such as the Exchange, the Library, the Museum, the Refectories, the Tower of Order, with belfry, clock and telegraph ; finally, the apartments, storehouses and offices of the Regency, or council chosen to administer unitarily the societary township.   Place in the different stories, and intermingle methodically the Seristeries and lodgings of all sorts, of all prices and all tastes, as much to avoid the present classification of our cities into *rich quarter* and *poor quarter*, as to facilitate the free play, the regular interlocking of the industrial series ; opposite this palace, on the other side of the main road, and at a proper distance, are the rural buildings"—

THE MOTHER. " It seems to me you forget the church."

X. "Not so, excuse me; I forget neither the temple nor the theatre : the temple in which to sing hymns to God ; the theatre in which to form men worthy to know and to adore the eternal Author of all things. But let us come to the education. You can conceive that, in an order of things in which groups of labor are freely and spontaneously formed, in which each can apply himself to those labors for which he has a taste and only to those, vocations and aptitudes must be manifested in a number exactly proportioned to our wants—some for cooking, some for sewing, some for administration, some for the sciences, some for the arts, some for the various functions of agriculture and of industry, some finally for the cares required by young children ; for God has strongly fixed the love of children in the hearts of certain women, and those women will passionately acquit themselves of the task for which they have a partiality, with the great applauses of the Phalanx which sees in those beloved shoots the prospect and the hope of its future success—of the Phalanx which will not fail to honor all those who apply themselves to education, Nurses, Bonnes and Teachers, and to recompense them as richly as they are poorly recompensed in our day. Not only will the Bonnes, the Nurses, give themselves up to their passion for children in general, but they will moreover attach themselves to those children whose natural character suits them ; some to the quiet children, others to the noisy ones. You can now understand, madam, how the different children of the Phalanx being brought up in groups, in very healthy halls, properly warmed, constantly visited by physicians interested in the preservation of the health of these little beings, it will be impossible for your son not to find exactly the Bonne who is fitted for him, one who will divine his wants, who will know how to bring him up, who will adopt yours in preference to every other ; while at present, chance and necessity being the only guides in the choice of Nurses and Bonnes, the most active maternal solicitude cannot fail to be often at fault.

"A Bonne who has a taste for her occupation can very well suffice for several children at once ; and God was doubtless right in willing that it should be so ; for if all children, like yours, required three or four persons, one half of the population would not be sufficient to bring up the other half; what time would they then have to apply themselves to other labors ?"

THE MOTHER. " You will perhaps consider it egotistical, sir, but I should wish to be able to bring up my children myself, by myself alone."

X. " It is a very excusable egotism, madam, the more so as you have at this day, no means of applying yourself to any other occupation. But with all your desire, all your discernment, with all your good will, are you very sure that you possess all the knowledges, and that you can command all the means, necessary for so difficult a task ?"

THE MOTHER. " Ah ! sir, it is my insufficiency that torments me."

X. " Well ! if you, madam, who unite so many qualities in this respect and in others, perceive that you still want some, if you confess that, in spite of your earnest and attentive vigilance, your children cannot be perfectly well brought up at home, by you, what must be the case with that multitude of women who, having received from God neither vocation nor aptitude for these functions, find the education of their own child not only difficult, but insupportable, or to whom society has refused the means and the leisure which your fortune enables you to devote to this occupation ? Nevertheless, our social order requires in all women the same aptitudes—and the most different, the most contrary aptitudes. What is the result ? The household goes on as it can, the education of children is very poor, and the women, already very much slaves in other respects, experience, owing to the complication and diversity of household labors, a subjection which all have not patience enough to bear."

THE MOTHER. " That is a great evil, without doubt ; but prudent and wise women must do away with it, by accomplishing holily their duties as wives and mothers."

X. " Eh ! madam, is it always in their power to accomplish them ? certainly, I am far from wishing to say a word against the respect that is due to duties ! But nevertheless, are not many of them merely conventional ? Do not judge other women by yourself, madam, or other households by yours. Yours is an entirely exceptional case. You like to stay at home, and your husband shares your tastes in this respect—the greatest quiet prevails in your house ; your children have, therefore, only excellent examples before their eyes. Both yourself and your husband, madam, naturally love the cares required by the education of your children ; neither of you having any taste for dissipation, you devote yourselves exclusively to those cares, and nothing of all this appears painful to you. In one word, you are in the most favorable condition. But transport yourself into those houses where the husband and wife, absolutely devoid of the taste and talents you possess, cannot agree respecting the method of education to be adopted, and still less respecting its execution ; go into those households where the married pair quarrel incessantly about the children, who, then, instead of drawing closer the conjugal bond, become on the contrary a perpetual occasion of discord ; try to penetrate into those families where are found only depraved manners and coarse words ; and see what examples are given, what principles are inculcated to those poor little ones ! It is said and often repeated that the natural teacher of the child is its mother ; that the cares of education, of the first education especially, are a sacred duty for the mother, a duty dictated by nature ; but if the mother has neither the character, nor the health, nor the talents necessary, what becomes, I ask you, of this idea of duty, which is doubtless a very beautiful thing in theory, but the practice of which leaves so much more to be desired as the duty is more contrary to the aptitudes, and agrees less with the organization of the individuals on whom it is imposed ?

"Suppose, in fact, that a child endowed with great genius is born of poor or ignorant parents ; how shall they bring up that child ? Does the heavy and stupid buzzard understand anything of the bold flight of the eagle ? With the best possible will to accomplish their duties, what will limited parents do in such a case ? They will treat as absurdities, as follies, the most sublime, the most elevated tendencies ; they will blast that genius at its birth. If you now consider what will become, at this day, of those unhappy children, whom death deprives of their father or their mother, sometimes of both, and of those, alas ! who never know to whom they owe their birth,—unfortunate beings, devoted to misfortune, to corruption, to crime, and about whom society never deigns to care until it brands them, punishes them for the inevitable consequences of their misery, of their deserted state, of their misfortune ; if you reflect that great numbers of parents, far from being able to attend to the education of their children, have not even wherewithal to provide them with their daily bread,—your heart as well as your understanding will convince you, madam, that God cannot have willed the education of children in the bosom of households as at present constituted, since this method presents the fewest happy chances and the greatest inconveniences for both parents and for children, and since, even while it is very onerous, it offers no guarantee either to society or to individuals."

THE MOTHER. "It is true that the lot of poor children is very precarious. But are there not halls of asylum ? are there not other establishments also ?"

X. "Yes, madam, these are partial ameliorations which it is desirable to encourage, so long as we are condemned to this *parcelled* régime ; but how insufficient, how powerless are these palliatives !"

THE MOTHER. "Excuse me, gentlemen, I am going to see if my son is asleep, I will return immediately—do not continue without me, I beg of you."

THE HUSBAND. "That is all very well, but the rich will say to you : 'What do I care for the children of others, provided my own are well educated ?'"

X. "I will reply to those rich persons : 'You are stupid and self-deceived, like all selfish people ; for I deny that your children can be well educated ; and besides, will they not suffer, during the whole of their lives, from the bad education, the grossness of others ?'"

THE MOTHER (returning). "He is asleep, gentlemen—sound asleep. Well ! sir, continue ; what you tell me is so full of interest, so new to me ! Continue, I beg of you."

X. "Willingly, madam.

"Three essential conditions must be observed in education : 1st. The development of the senses ; 2d. The development of characters and vocations ; 3d. The intellectual development.

"You will shortly be convinced, madam, that the methods used, let us rather say, the means to which civilization is reduced, far from satisfying these three conditions, these three aims of education, do not even propose to attain them.

"It is easy to understand that, in the case of the youngest children, the present régime acts without consulting the convenience of parents. If they are rich enough to be able to bring up their children under their own eyes, they necessarily become their slaves. Obliged to seclude themselves, to deprive themselves of the sight of their friends, in order that they may devote their whole time exclusively to the education of their children, they have the sorrow of not being able to succeed even in this. If they are compelled by their business to be absent, they are obliged to confide their children to corrupt domestics.

"So much for rich parents. As for those who are not in easy circumstances, they are forced to separate from their children, to confide them to mercenary women whom they do not know, and who never fail to deceive them.

"The present régime, I said, consults no more the convenience of the children than that of the persons called upon to take care of them, to bring them up. Does any one think, in families, does any one think, in houses of education, to refine the senses, the taste, the smell, the touch ? By no means ; and as to the hearing, far from studying to refine this sense, one would say that children are placed in circumstances made on purpose to falsify both their ear and their voice ! Examine closely all the consequences of the usages followed in this respect, and you will easily perceive to how many physical and moral deformities we are exposed from our tenderest years, owing to the objects and the persons that surround us.

"But you are already informed of the culpable carelessness which our society displays towards children, as well as towards all members of the social body. Do you wish to have an idea of the foresight of the societary order? listen to Fourier:

"'Civilization, always *simplistic*, or simple in its methods, knows only the cradle as a receptacle for the nursing child. Harmony, which operates in the *composite* order, gives two situations to the child; it makes him alternate from the cradle to the elastic mat. These mats are placed about breast high ; their supports form hollows, in which each child can find a place without troubling his neighbors. Nets of cord or silk, placed from distance to distance, enclose the child, without preventing him from moving or seeing round about him, and approaching the neighboring child, from whom he is separated by a net.

"'The hall is warmed to the degree proper for keeping the child in light clothing, and avoiding the inconveniences of swaddling clothes and furs. The cradles are moved by machinery; twenty can be vibrated at a time. A single child will perform this service, which among us would occupy twenty women.

"'The nurses constitute a distinct series, and must be classed according to temperament, in order that they may be assorted to the children, especially in the case of a change of milk. Indirect nursing is much practised in Harmony, because it is very lucrative and not very fatiguing, and because the Harmonians, more judicious than Jean Jacques Rousseau, think that, when the mother is of a delicate complexion, it is very prudent to give to the child a robust nurse; this is *grafting* him, reinforcing him. Nature wishes these crossings. If we fasten a weak child to a weak mother, we only injure the health of both for the honor of a moral revery. Moreover, great attention will be paid to perfecting the system of artificial nursing, and employing it in concurrence with the natural, or alone. In the societary state, no mother, however opulent she may be, can ever think of bringing up her child at home isolatedly; he would not there receive a quarter part of the attentions he finds at the seristery of the babies or nursing children; and, with every imaginable expenditure, no one could assemble in her own house a corporation of intelligent *empassioned Bonnes*, relaying each other incessantly, in three characters assorted to the children. A princess, in spite of every expenditure, could not have halls so carefully attended to, elastic mats, with the neighborhood of children, who serve as a reciprocal distraction, and are assorted in characters. It is principally in this education of the first infancy that we recognise how far the richest civilized potentate falls short of the means which Harmony lavishes upon the poorest fathers and children.

"'Far from this, everything is arranged in civilization so that the nursing child is the torment of a house organized to torment him. The child, without knowing it, desires the arrangements he would find in a seristery of Harmony, for want of which he annoys by his cries parents, servants and neighbors, all the while injuring his own health.

"'At six months old, when we do not think of giving the least instruction to our little monkeys, numerous precautions will be taken to form and to refine their senses, to mould them to dexterity, to prevent the exclusive use of one hand and one arm, which condemns the other arm to a perpetual awkwardness; to accustom the child from his cradle to justness of ear, by having duets and quartettes sung in the halls of the nursing babies, and by walking about with children of a year old to the sound of a little flourish of all instruments. There will also be methods of joining the refinement of hearing to musical refinement, in order to give to children the fineness of ear possessed by the rhinoceros, and the Cossack, and to exercise the other senses in the same manner. Hence the societary child at three years old will be more intelligent, better fitted for industry, than are at ten many civilized children, who at that age have only an antipathy for industry and the arts.

"'The part of Bonne will therefore require numerous talents, and will not be limited, as in France, to singing false and making children afraid of the wolf. The Bonnes will especially exert themselves to prevent the cries of the children; calmness is necessary to them; it will be upon the art of preserving this that the cabalistic and emulative pretensions will be exercised.

"'The uproar of little children, so grievous in our day, will be reduced to a small matter; they will be much softened in the seristeries; and a well known reason for this is, that quarrelsome characters become humanized with those who are like them. Do we not every day see fencers and bullies become very gentle, and give up their overbearing humor when in the company of their equals? It will be the same with the children brought up in the seristeries of Harmony, and distributed in several halls according to character. I calculate that those of the third class, the little devils and demoniacs, will already be less wicked, less screamers than are now the benign ones. Whence will proceed this softening? Shall we, according to the desire of moral philosophy, have *changed the passions of those little children?* No, certainly; they will have been developed without excess by procuring for them the relaxations of sympathetic assemblages.'"[*]

THE MOTHER. "Yes, I do believe, in fact, that the children would be more happy so. But what will you do with them afterwards?"

X. "In proportion as the child grows older, you are aware that the inconveniences and the difficulties of our present education become still more numerous. The need of action, of emulation,

* Nouveau Monde Industriel, 2d edit., p. 174, et seq.

the instinctive desire of acquiring knowledge, that uneasy curiosity which leads children to inquire, to learn—all those precious qualities which you have *compressed* with such great pains, years *develop* them in spite of you; years awaken in them the necessity of finding themselves in the midst of their companions, of their equals; if this necessity is not satisfied (and a home education cannot satisfy it), then they are a perpetual torment; they become noisy, turbulent; the want of industrial exercise makes them awkward; they tear and break everything; they wear you out; they ask you very embarrassing questions, and overwhelm you with their indiscretions. In order to avoid their indiscretions, and to elude their sagacity, you are compelled to restrain yourself, to keep watch over your words, your slightest actions, and even sometimes to lie to them."

THE HUSBAND. "Oh! yes, that is true, quite true; and my wife could mention to you two or three recent circumstances in which she was greatly embarrassed by the indiscretion of our little Mary. What a terrible child she is! we always have to distrust her; when we think she is very busy with her playthings, it is exactly then that she is listening most attentively to everything that is said."

X. "Well! could you not turn to some use this curiosity against which you are obliged to be always on your guard? Instead of applying all your cares to elude it, could you not make it serve for education? Poor children! how much trouble do parents take to check this sap, to turn back this exuberance of life which God has placed in them!

"Ah! certainly there is something false here which should not be, something which indicates to you that the domestic hearth is not the place which is fitted, or at least which is sufficient for the child."

THE HUSBAND. "How you go on! But that sap, that exuberance—if it were not checked, do you know what would happen?"

X. "It would happen that, abandoned to themselves, children would commit bad actions."

THE HUSBAND. "Crimes even!"

X. "Yes; that is seen, that takes place every day, in spite of the compression which is exercised upon them, and sometimes in consequence of that very compression. Poor children! so well made for order, justice, truth, for all the Harmonies; in whom the feeling of harmony is so powerful, because they are nearer than ourselves to nature! Poor children! what a pity that the medium in which they are placed so falsifies them! What a pity that society stifles by degrees so many beautiful and noble instincts!"

THE MOTHER. "And you believe——?"

X. "I believe, madam, that, as soon as we shall know how to amuse children with useful things, as soon as we shall have created for them *attractive education*, they will no longer seek excitements of the subversive order. But, in our day, to blame them for this would be:—It would be acting like one of my cousins with his son, a charming child: when his father *moralizes* him, and accuses him with being lazy, the poor child thinks he is very wrong; and because Greek and Latin are given to him to digest, when he, the child, would wish to be running in the fields after the sheep and cows, he cries, and promises to amend, to correct himself, that is to falsify himself, to like Greek and Latin, when he was born to live in the middle of the fields. Vain promise! nature is stronger than the will. Thus do you know what the child says to me when I am alone with him? 'It is very hard, it is, cousin, to be a lazy little fellow like me; when I am not studying, I am contented—and I am not contented—' Honest and intelligent child! He instinctively comprehends the struggle which exists between his tastes and the duties that are imposed upon him."

MYSELF. "And which are necessarily imposed upon him, for it is impossible, in our day, to bring up children without compressing, without falsifying them."

THE MOTHER. "And yet with good principles, a good direction—"

X. "Eh! how will you direct them?"

THE MOTHER. "In the way that our experience and our solicitude shall suggest to us; and you may trust us for that."

X. "Excuse me, madam; but, without practical means—experience, solicitude and all the good principles in the world are perfectly useless. You think you have done everything when you have impressed upon your children the direction which you deem preferable for them ; and you do not see that this arbitrary direction, instead of turning to the advantage of your children, is to them a source of *falsification* and real servitude."

THE MOTHER. " But no ! our intention is not to constrain them ; on the contrary, we shall let them choose."

X. " Can they ? do you place them in a situation to do so ?"

THE MOTHER. " Eh ! who, better than the parents, can tell what is most proper for their children ?"

X. " The children themselves, madam. But it is not by remaining incessantly under the eyes of his parents, it is not by seeing always the same objects, that the child can learn to know his vocation, or rather his *vocations*. He must be placed in the midst of all objects having relation to the arts and sciences, to industry ; he must be placed in the midst of other children, whose manias, tastes and rivalries he will espouse ; otherwise he will be twenty or thirty years old without feeling any determined taste. And if at that age the slumbering vocation awakens under the influence of the liberty which you permit him to enjoy, alas ! it is too late ! and this knowledge can only occasion him regret."

THE HUSBAND. " But, my friend, you see that children find their vocations no better at college than at home."

X. " Eh ! doubtless, because, at college, that which I have just spoken of is not done. A college education, though better than a home education, is none the less insufficient and absurd ; theory is there made to take precedence of practice ; children are expected to comprehend the utility of an abstraction, of a principle, of which they are not even shown the application. And then, how can they be expected to make real progress ? they are kept until twenty upon books, exclusively upon books, without being made to do anything that has a relation to social things ; they are placed completely outside of society, while from four years old they might, they ought to, be connected with it by their labors, their studies, their amusements.

" The college education is vicious and incomplete ; who denies it ? Who would dare to deny that, at college, children find evil examples ; that they there contract pernicious habits ? Do we not know that they there find none of the attentions which their age requires? And how can it be otherwise? Colleges and boarding schools are generally exploited by speculators who want means, who want knowledge, or by administrators who do not imagine the immensity of their mission, and to whom moreover nothing that is necessary to accomplish it is supplied.

" A great obstacle to the success of education, you must know, is that no one ever seeks to develop in the child more than one vocation at once, while he indubitably possesses a certain number which should be developed by means of each other. In truth, if in Harmony all the vocations find their satisfaction in the variety of labors, in Civilization, where labor is not organized, where no bond exists between the different branches of industry, a man can select only one function, to the exclusion of all others; he must choose a specialty; he must indeed, for fear of failure, conform to that sad and absurd proverb, a true *civilizee* proverb: 'Do not hunt two hares at once.' Now, instead of hunting two hares at once, our teachers do not even try to hunt a single one; they do not imagine the least in the world that the essential aim, or more correctly, the only aim of education, is the development of vocations, a development without which every education is necessarily a failure. When, by a great expenditure of *pensums,* they have made their pupils learn the rudiments, the regulation of the participles, the ellipsis, when they have taught them Greek and Latin, philosophy, rhetoric; when they have stuffed their head with the most contradictory principles; then they imagine that they have made men. Singular illusion! Therefore they gather almost no fruit from their pains; therefore the career of teaching, dry, wearisome, as much for the professors as for the children, is forsaken by almost all men of any worth. In Harmony, on the contrary, the elect of the savans consider it an honor as well as a pleasure to form part of the teaching body. There, the pupil, instead of being reduced to a single master, according to the arrangements of the present régime, finds masters of every age, of every character, whose scientific tastes he espouses passionately and freely, in proportion as those tastes are in conformity with his own; masters who, not only by the variety of their knowledges and their aptitudes, but moreover by all the means which the Phalanx takes care to place at their disposal, possess elements of success infinitely superior to those of our first royal colleges, and out of all proportion with those which can be commanded by any mother of a family, the most devoted, the best fitted for such an occupation.

"In education as in agriculture, as in industry, the great evil, the great sore, is *parcelling*. The same means, the same resources, the same knowledges that are wanting to the peasant on his farm, are wanting to the industrialist in his workshop, to the family in its household, and to teachers in their colleges or boarding schools.

"The teachers limit themselves, I repeat, to paying attention to intellectual education; less than this, to purely literary education; and they do not see that, under penalty of failing, as they do, with seven-eighths of the children, under penalty of finding in all more or less vivid repugnances, of deteriorating the frankest characters, of blasting the most fruitful minds, it is necessary first to develop the senses, and then to pay attention at the same time to the vocations and to instruction. Well! no! willing or unwilling, they wish to force children to accept theory before practice, or rather without practice; for, far from profiting by the activity of their pupils, they prevent them from applying themselves to any exercise; they reduce to the condition of automatons those little beings so full of life, of fire and of growing passions. Poor children! who have so great a need of movement! who ask only the free air to open in and the sun to strengthen them, they are shut up for ten hours a day, they are deprived of air, of movement and of sun! What is the case then when we think of the children of the poor, of those little unfortunates whom our factories keep imprisoned for sixteen hours, in the midst of a mephitic atmosphere? And then they complain that all children are rebellious, indocile, noisy, wicked!—but the best dog, if he is too much irritated, will bite his master. And then it is a matter of astonishment that their bodies are diseased, their minds weak!—but a flower which is bent, under pretext of forming it, fades and dies!

"In home education, the same system, and still more serious

inconveniences! If the parents had fifty thousand francs income, they could not bring together in their house, even the weakest elements of success that are found in a college. In the family, there is no rivalry, no emulation for the child! In the family, the development of vocations is completely impossible. Admitting (which is never found to be the case) that the father and mother possess all possible knowledges, they may not be apt at teaching: for it is one thing to know and another thing to teach. Will they take professors at so much the lesson? For this purpose they must live in a large city. A single professor lodging with them? Alas! who does not know the inconveniences and the insufficiency of both these methods? And then, if by a miracle they have firmness enough, enough power over themselves to avoid the danger of *spoiling* (a danger so imminent in domestic education), they fall into the opposite excess; and the chastisements which they inflict make them lose the affection of their child; so that, instead of producing happiness, instead of bringing closer the bonds of affection in a family, as is generally believed, a home education is often, on the contrary, a source of ennuis, of cool-ness, of disaffection between the father and the child.

"What a difference in Harmony! All the difficulties with which education is surrounded in our day, disappear to give place to a mechanism so simple that it seems to work of itself. There, there is a providence for little children, as there is a providence for men; there, EVERY child has a right to education, to *attractive* education; for it is in amusing himself, in taking exercise with the children of his own age, it is in receiving, or rather, in soliciting lessons from his elders, that the child is taught, that he obtains grades, distinctions, that he earns his dividends, and takes rank in the great human family! Thus you see, as in our day it is chance which delivers a child to such a nurse, to such a bonne, and later in life places him under the ferule of a master for whom he feels no sympathy; so in Harmony, the affectionate selections which you have seen to prevail on the part of the bonne towards the child, also take place on the part of the master towards the pupil. The greatest liberty is granted to both. There is no other rule than the *attraction* which draws one towards the other; and as the child is incessantly placed in connexion with the per-

2

sons, in contact with the objects which may *attract* him; as he has under his hand all the instruments of labor, under his eyes all the practical lessons which may awaken his inclinations, flatter his tastes, excite his imitative mania, he attains naturally and necessarily to the most complete development of his vocations; that is the great affair in Harmony; a vocation lost or smothered would be a note dropped in the social concert. But the phalansterian régime provides so well for everything, that not a man of merit will be unrecognised, no great talent will be lost, no capacity will be smothered, unknown, not one will be ignorant of its own existence, and men of genius will be as numerous as they are rare in our day. Thus Fourier, comprehending all the importance of this question, has examined and analysed with the greatest care the springs which nature wishes to put in motion in order to lead children to industry.

"'The dominant tastes in all children,' he says, 'are,

"'1st. FERRETING, or inclination to handle everything, to visit everything, to examine everything, to vary occupation incessantly.

"'2d. Industrial *uproar*, taste for noisy labors.

"'3d. *Monkery*, or imitative mania.

"'4th. *Miniature* industry, love for little workshops.

"'5th. PROGRESSIVE ATTRACTION, from the weak to the strong.'

"Then, seeking for the methods to be followed in order to apply these tastes from the earliest age, he reckons twenty-four allurements or springs for the development of vocations."

THE FATHER. "All this is very well; but I don't see when and how the children will study."

X. "Fourier explains it to you:

"'Studies will figure only in the second order; they must have their origin in a curiosity awakened by material occupations. The labor of the school must be united to that of the workshops and cultivation, and excited by the impressions received in those workshops.

"'For instance, Nisus, at six years old, is empassioned for the care of pheasants and pinks; he figures actively in the intrigues of the groups which take care of the pheasantry and the pink beds.

"'In order to introduce Nisus into the schools, they will take good care not to put in play paternal authority, the fear of ferules, or even the hope of reward.' They wish, on the contrary, to lead Nisus and his companions to ask for instruction : how shall this be done ? The senses, which are the guides of the child, must be allured.

"' The Venerable Theophrastus, who at the pheasantry presides over the Cherubins (the name of the second infantile tribe), and assists them with his advice, will bring to the meeting a big book containing engravings of different species of pheasants, of those which the canton possesses, and of those which it does not possess. (This is a volume of the illustrated Naturalogical Encyclopædia.)

"' These engravings are the delight of children five years old ; they eagerly go over the collection. Beneath each of these *beautiful images* is a short definition. Two or three of them are explained to the children ; they would like to have all the others read, but the Venerable of the station, or the Seraphin of the round have *not time enough* to bestow upon these explanations.

"' This is a ruse agreed upon in the seristeries of the younger childhood ; all agree in telling the Cherubin that they have no time to explain to him what he wishes to know, they adroitly refuse to him the instruction he asks for ; he is told that if he wishes to know so many things, he has only to learn to read like such and such a one, who are no older than he, and who, knowing how to read, are already admitted to the lesser library.

"' Thereupon, the Seraphin carries away the book with the *beautiful images*, which is wanted in the halls of study. The same ruse is practised with the children who cultivate pinks : their curiosity has been excited without being fully satisfied.

"' Nisus, piqued by the double privation he has endured at the groups of the pheasantry and the pink beds, wishes to learn to read that he may obtain admittance to the library, in order to see there the big books which contain so many *beautiful images*. Nisus communicates his project to his friend Euryalus, and both form the noble plot of learning to read. When the intention is once awakened and manifested, they will find assistance enough from teaching ; but the societary state wishes to lead them to *ask for instruction ;* their progress will be three-fold more rapid when study shall be a *labor of attraction*, a *solicited teaching.*

"' Here I have brought into play one of the favorite tastes of childhood, the taste for illuminated engravings, representing the objects in which the child is strongly interested from their connexions with his labors.

"' This spring seems sufficient to awaken the idea of learning to read : let us more thoroughly analyse the allurement, and distinguish in it a bi-composite moving power, double in material, and double in spiritual.

" ' In material : 1st, the impatience to know the explanation of so many *beautiful images ;* 2d, the connexion of those engravings with the animals or vegetables which he takes care of from preference ;

" ' In spiritual : 3d, the desire of rising from the sub-choir of the mi-cherubins to the sub-choir of high-cherubins, who will not receive him unless he knows how to read ; 4th, the irony of several of the high-cherubins, who, already knowing how to read, laugh at those who are behindhand.

" ' Put in play these vehicles of bi-composite attraction, and the success will be as speedy as it would be slow and doubtful, if recurrence were had to civilizee moving powers, to the commands of the father or schoolmaster, to penances and punishments, or to the weak attractions of some of our present methods, the most praised of which, *mutualism,* does not even attain to the degree of composite vehicle, much less bi-composite.

" ' The same method will prevail in the various branches of study, writing, grammar, &c. They will always introduce the bi-composite allurement, concerted refusals and innocent ruses, to excite emulation. It can be produced only upon branches of studies analogous to the labors which the child exercises passion-ately. It is, therefore, in every point of view, by the material of industry that his education must commence, and nothing is more misconceived than the *simplistic* method of the Civilizees, who wish to make a child a geometrician, a chemist, before having allured him to the occupations fitted to awaken in him the desire of knowing mathematics and chemistry, and of combining these theories with the practice by which he has commenced.'*

"There, madam, look at your children ; just now they were playing on the carpet ; now they have changed their occupation. Do not disturb them : let us take Nature in the very act. Now they are at work building a machine ; a very important occupa-tion, which requires all their attention—Do they always agree ?

THE MOTHER. "Yes, quite well."

X. "I congratulate you on it, madam. It is a great chance and a great happiness for you ; for the family household offers few resources for the development of elective affinities ; therefore we

* Theory of Universal Unity, vol. iv., p. 119.

often see brothers quarrel among themselves. See with what ardor your children work upon that machine. Very soon they will be tired, they will busy themselves with something else ; but you will remark, if you provide them with the means, that they will apply themselves from preference to useful occupations, having some connexion with industrial and social relations, with things they may have observed, and which they are naturally led to imitate ; and if you interest their self-love, if you know how to give importance to their most trifling labors, you will see how proud they will be of their co-operation, and how anxious they will be to offer you their little services."

THE MOTHER. " The little rogues show no such ardor in learning to read."

X. " That is easily understood ; they do not see the use of it. But let them perceive the object of anything, and if that thing is to their taste, you will see with what enthusiasm they will undertake it."

THE MOTHER. " Oh ! you are right."

X. " To put children in a situation in which they can fulfil the various functions which interest them, to excite their enthusiasm by exaggerating the importance of small things—herein is contained the whole secret of education and instruction. They say that children are lazy, that they love nothing but play, waste, amusements ; that they are devoid of industrial faculties. What experiments have been made to ascertain if this be true ? But no ! it is enough to observe children in order to be satisfied that completely the contrary is the case. · How many times, when I was young (and certainly I was what is called a dissipated child, a real blackguard, I am proud of it ! ardent at play, ardent in running, always in mud and water), how many times did I refuse a game at bars, at top, or at ball, to continue an industrial occupation which pleased me, which attracted me ! There, do you hear those babies gravely discussing the advantage of placing such a piece rather than another ? The youngest boy wishes to demonstrate to the oldest ; this is an exceptional case, for usually the younger have a great deal of veneration for their elders ; they listen to their instructions as men listen to oracles ; but this fact is explained by the great difference of age which exists between these children, a thing which is inevitable in the *parcelled* household."

THE MOTHER. "But, Sir, the one whom you call the youngest boy is a girl, it is my little Mary."

X. "Ah! then I understand, I understand—and I congratulate you so much the more on the good agreement which prevails between them. You ought to rejoice that your children, though differing in age and sex, possess affinitary characters, which are not generally found except in a certain number of individuals; this is an advantage which can rarely be enjoyed but in the *societary* household."

THE MOTHER. "Oh! Sir, there are really great differences in their characters and their tastes; if I should let my son do as he wishes, he would be always in the dirt."

X. "Well!"

THE MOTHER. "While his sister displays a coquetry which frightens me."

X. "Very well!"

THE MOTHER. "When she is dressing her doll, her brother must not disturb her. And when we are to go out, you cannot imagine what minute attention she bestows upon her toilet, how important it is to her; she examines her collar; she examines her hair—ah! I am very much disturbed at it, I fear she has a taste for coquetry."

X. "Eh! madam, perhaps you will not believe me; but, really, you complain because your children are too well endowed. In Harmony, the taste for dirt and the taste for dress are the most profitable possible; but, at this day, when they can only have an *inharmonic* application, I understand your anxiety."

THE MOTHER. "What must I do, then?"

X. "I confess, madam, that mothers of families are placed in a situation of great embarrassment—On the one hand, endeavor to prevent these tastes from being too much developed, since they may be fatal at present; on the other, take care not to falsify the minds of your children, make them as little unhappy as possible, watch over them as well as you can; finally, do all that is in your power, and be resigned to anything unpleasant that may happen to them—this is the only advice I can give you for the moment."

THE MOTHER. "Have you advice, then, only for the future ?"

X. "Alas! yes, madam; but we point out the means of making that future become present to-morrow, if men are willing."

THE MOTHER. "Let them begin at once then !"

X. "Ah! madam, the men who preside over our destinies, the sophists who rule opinion, and I must say, the immense majority of the public who listen to those sophists, much prefer busying themselves about electoral reforms and similar stupidities. This is much more amusing, much more attractive, much better fitted to secure the happiness of the nation! Poor France! Poor Humanity! The saddest part of the matter is to see our journalists maintain the public in these illusions, at least as much as they can; but the public begin to be a little tired of them. I don't remember who it was told me the other day that the public taste required henceforth a daily feuilleton* in the daily journals. For myself I don't know if the *taste* of the public has anything to do with it; but I see with pleasure that their *disgust* with politics has a great deal."

At this moment, by some awkwardness on the part of the little boy, the machine was overturned, and there arose, between the two children, an altercation, which they hastened to submit to their mother. It was quite a curious spectacle to see the warmth displayed by each in defending its right. The mother cut short the difficulty by asking both if they knew their lesson.

" Yes, mamma," said Mary.

" I have not had time," said the brother, with a pouting air.

THE MOTHER. " How is that, you lazy fellow! you have had time enough to make machines."

THE LITTLE BOY. " Why! mamma, it amuses me to make machines. You think it is amusing to study; I assure you it is not."

THE MOTHER. " How, how! you little arguer !"

THE LITTLE BOY. " But yes, mamma, if it was amusing I should like it; but it is wearisome, I do not—"

* The feuilleton is that portion of the French journals which contains the novel, or romance, now so generally published in those papers.

THE MOTHER. "How is this, sir! must your task be amusing to you for you to work?"

THE LITTLE BOY. "Why!"—

THE MOTHER. "Go, sir; go at once into your father's study, by yourself, until you know your two fables. Then you will come and recite them to me."

The child retired with tears in his eyes. As to the mother, the effort she had just made to punish her son, proved to us very clearly that this obligation is not in nature.

II.

X. "I am sorry to tell you, madam—or rather I am happy to make the remark to you—there is great good sense in your son's words. It is Nature herself who has spoken by his mouth; it is Nature who has just given a lesson to our notions, our prejudices. We are so accustomed to find repugnance in our occupations, that we cannot unite the idea of *pleasure* with that of *labor*. Well! that child, who is not falsified as we are, has just told us artlessly what Nature inspires him: I should love my duty, if my duty were more loveable. It is you, therefore, who are wrong, madam, and it is your son who is right. And yet you call him lazy. Was he lazy, just now, at play, at his machine? Well! madam, the argument you have just used with your son is that of civilizee fathers in general. They refer everything to themselves; they judge of everything according to the proprieties of our society, and whenever their children depart in the least from the line they have traced out for them, they hasten to condemn them. The other day a grave, judicious man held with me, respecting his son, the following discourse, which I would not have believed had I not heard it: 'My son,' said he to me, 'is an idle fellow! Would you believe, sir, that after having gone through his studies, he was not willing either to become a lawyer or to enter the magistracy? In the first place he studied mathematics; now he is studying botany, anatomy; he wishes to learn medicine. When he is a doctor, do you think that he will practise, that he will fix himself at last in an honorable profession? By no means; he will amuse himself with something else. Oh! I am greatly grieved, my son is an idle fellow who will never do anything.' What praise there was, madam, in this paternal censure! It gave me the desire to become a friend of that idle fellow; I shall certainly make an excellent Phalansterian of him. What an elevated character! What a noble and vast intellect! How precious would he be in Harmony! And how such brilliant faculties, such different aptitudes, would find, in a Phalanstery, an application useful to society and profitable to the individual!"

THE MOTHER. "That is possible; but in the meanwhile, sir, you must allow that the father was in a measure right, and that the result is rather a sad one for him."

X. "Excuse me, madam; he would be right in complaining that our social order condemns the most eminent minds to uselessness, to inaction; but the father is wrong in blaming his son for this deplorable result."

THE HUSBAND. "My dear sir, if you were a father, you would understand—"

X. "What?—I should understand that the future lot of children is a very embarrassing thing—yes, no doubt."

THE MOTHER. "And full of anxiety, sir. You will perhaps consider me foolish, but I assure you that I am already asking myself with anxiety what career I shall choose for my children."

X. "That does not astonish me, madam, since you have no means of divining that in which your children have the greatest chance of success. Eh! it is thus that in our day no one can enjoy that carelessness to which we all aspire. Carelessness! it is not even permitted to little children!"

THE MOTHER. "How! carelessness? But I should not wish my children to be careless. It seems to me that carelessness belongs to persons who have no taste for anything, who take things as they happen."

X. "Perhaps the word is not very well chosen here, since, in fact, the definition which you give to it, madam, is the only one generally received. The language is poor; and yet there are such loud exclamations whenever a man ventures to create a new word! I mean by carelessness the absence of care, of anxiety for the morrow. *Care for the morrow!* but it is a perpetual nightmare, from which the richest are not exempt, a nightmare from which even little children are not spared. For instance, a few days since, I was at a friend's house; his son, five or six years old, was there, near us, silent. We looked at him; his eye was fixed, his eyelids lowered; and by the intellectual labor that was going on in that little brain you would have said the head would burst. 'What are you thinking of, my little Jules?' asked his father. 'What am I thinking of?' replied the child; 'I am thinking how I shall support you, when I am great and you are little.'"

THE MOTHER. "Poor little thing! How I should have kissed him."

X. "That is what the father did not fail to do."

THE MOTHER. "Well! sir, mine sometimes make such reflections; really, I assure you, they often make me ponder on many things."

X. "I believe it, madam; children—I mean quite young children, those whose precocious intellects there has as yet been no opportunity to falsify, have a great deal more good sense than their parents and teachers. Those teachers have published volumes of proverbs which are called *The Wisdom of Nations;* they would have done much better to have collected the reflections, the repartees of their pupils, and composed of them a book entitled, *The Wisdom of Children,* or rather, *The Wisdom of Nature.*

"Allow me to mention to you yet another of those sayings, great in naïveté, in simplicity. Last evening I was in a public place where two gentlemen were discussing an important question, viz: 'That it would be very desirable to invent a machine for shaving, which would relieve the bearded sex from the ennui of lather and the barber.' 'But, papa,' said a child, who was following the conversation with great blue eyes wide open and very intelligent, 'suppose people should not shave themselves at all?' 'What is that you are saying?' 'Why!' added the child, 'since people have beards, they are not made to be shaved off.' 'Is the child a fool?' 'Not so much of a fool, either,' ventured the other speaker, 'the fact is that a beard gives to a man's physiognomy a character which it would otherwise want.' 'Oh!' said the father, laughing, ' but if I did not shave, my wife would think my beard too hard—' and there the conversation ended. 'Yes,' said I, jestingly, to a friend who was listening with me, ' she would think it too hard for a fortnight, but try to keep it three months—'

"But I am continually wandering from my subject: *Opposition of the present education to Nature and to good sense*, such is in a few words the result of our methods of education. Private education is insufficient and false ; it smothers the faculties and the instincts of the child, by isolating him, by refusing to him companions for his plays; it falsifies his character, it is opposed to the free development of his vocations. As to public education, we have said enough to show its insufficiency and its inconveniences of every species ; and, as to its falseness, I desire no other proof than a saying you may have read beneath one of Charlet's caricatures, a saying which would figure very well in the book of *The Wisdom of Children*. The caricature represents a boy, satchel over shoulder, going sadly to school, scratching his head : 'If I were the government,' says he, 'I would have everybody *know* how to read, so that there *may be* no schoolmasters.' In this repugnance of the child, there is a whole revelation.

" Moreover, it is generally acknowledged that in the falseness, in the insufficiency of our present education, is found one of the great causes of our social miseries ; but no one, yes, no one, has pointed out the remedy, except Fourier. 'From the age of five years,' says he, ' civilization begins to stuff the minds of children with *healthy doctrines*, which deform their characters, especially those of women.' I see, madam, that these words, *healthy doctrines*, used by Fourier in an unfavorable sense, astonish and shock you. Listen to the following passage from our master, and your astonishment will cease."

X. drew from his pocket a thick volume, and began to read :

" ' The further we advance in the examination of harmonian education, the more shall we recognise this *opposition of moral philosophy to nature* : it is well to recapitulate here some of the details drawn from the education of earlier childhood.

" ' Moral philosophy wishes to base the system of education for little children upon the smallest domestic assemblage, that of the conjugal household. Nature wishes to base this education upon the largest domestic combination, distributed in three degrees: groups, series of groups, and the phalanx of series. Outside of this vast assemblage it is impossible either to form the two scales of functions, and of functionaries acting in emulation upon each portion of the scale, or to satisfy in children the character and the temperament which require the halls and the services annexed to this double scale, services impracticable except in a phalanx of industrial series. · Thus, in a family household, the child is so wearied as to scream day and night, without either himself or his parents being able to imagine the distractions which he requires, and which he would find in a seristery of early childhood.

" ' Moral philosophy wishes that, in this family household, the father shall be delighted to hear the perpetual uproar of little monkeys, who deprive him of sleep, and disturb his labor. Nature, on the contrary, wishes that every man, poor as well as rich, may be delivered from this moral hubbub, and that, restored to his dignity, he may remove to some distant location that diabolical brood, place the children in a situation where they can be healthily and agreeably kept, according to the societary method which assures the rest of fathers, of mothers, of children ; they are all harassed by the civilized régime, called sweet household, a real hell for the people, when there is neither a separate apartment for the children, nor money to supply their wants.

" ' Moral philosophy wishes that the mother shall nurse her child, which is a very useless precept for poor mothers, who constitute seven-eighths ; far from having wherewithal to pay for a nurse, they endeavor to obtain nursing children who will pay them. As to the rich mothers, to the number of one-eighth, this function should be forbidden them, for they are the *assassins* of the child. From want of occupation, they study to create in him a thousand hurtful fancies, which are a slow poison, and kill the greater part of rich children.

" ' People are incessantly astonished at death's taking away the only son of a wealthy house, while it spares in the hovels the wretched children, deprived of bread ; those little village monkeys have a guarantee of health in the poverty of their mother, who, obliged to go to work in the fields, has no time to busy herself with their whims, and still less to create them, as does the lady of the chateau. Thus Jean Jacques Rousseau, while thinking to recall mothers to the tender feelings of tender moral philosophy, introduced the fashion of nursing among the very class of women who should have been excluded from it ; for, in that rich class they usually want, either the necessary health, or the cold and prudent character which would preserve both mother and child from injury.'"

THE MOTHER. "Eh! what, Sir, does not Fourier wish to have mothers nurse their own children? nevertheless—

X. "We will return to that point immediately, madam ; but before doing so, allow me to finish this astonishing passage in which Fourier does such prompt and good justice to a host of the *pretended moral* prescriptions of moral philosophy."

"'Moral philosophy forbids the father to spoil his child ; this, on the contrary, is the only function reserved to the father, his child being sufficiently criticised and lectured in the societary régime, by the groups of which he forms a part, or, if he is very small, by the Bonnes who take care of him in the Seristeries of early childhood.

"'Moral philosophy wishes the father to be the natural teacher of the child ; this is a task from which nature excludes him, and which she reserves to the *Bonnins* and *Mentorins* (names given by Fourier to the teachers of 2d and 3d degree), persons formed for this function by instinct and the corporative spirit.

"'Moral philosophy wishes to place around the child some half dozen grandmothers and aunts, sisters and cousins, neighbors and gossips, to create in him fancies which injure his health, and to falsify his ear with French music. Nature wishes that not the twentieth part of this apparatus shall be employed to keep the child healthy and gay in a Seristery assorted for all the instincts of his early years.

"'Moral philosophy wishes the child to be brought up from his tenderest years to despise riches and to esteem the shop-keepers. Nature wishes, on the contrary, that the child be early brought up to esteem money, and to exert himself to acquire it by the practice of truth, which, in civilization, cannot lead to riches, and which is incompatible with inverse commerce, the present system.

"'Moral philosophy wishes that no refined tastes should be allowed to children, especially in gourmandism, and that they should eat indifferently everything that is put before them. Nature wishes them to be brought up to gastronomic requirements, to the refinements of this art, which, in Harmony, becomes a direct means of impassioning them for agriculture.

"'It is therefore certain that moral philosophy, even supposing it has good intentions, plays the part of an ignorant physician, who gives only pernicious advice, knows only how to thwart the views of nature, and to kill his patients with a display of fine doctrines.' *

"What do you think of that passage ?"

THE HUSBAND. "It is very curious certainly; I don't know that good arguments could not be found to oppose some of the criticisms you have read, but, assuredly, there are some of striking justness.   Please to mark the passage, and to leave the book with me for two or three days; I shall be delighted to read that series of accusations attentively, and to weigh each of them."

X. "Very well, my friend, meditate, I beseech you, upon this beautiful criticism of so many stupidities which are still in favor. But let us listen to madam ; she had some observations to make respecting the nursing of a child by its mother."

THE MOTHER. "Yes, Sir ; I do not conceal from you that I am entirely of Rousseau's opinion ; a mother *ought* to nurse her children ; it is for her a *duty*, to the accomplishment of which, moreover, nature has attached so many charms ! I nursed my two eldest, and if I did surrender my last to the bosom of a stranger, believe me, Sir, it was entirely against my will ; a formal order of the physicians was necessary to require me to make this sacrifice ; and then I was not resigned until after many difficulties."

THE HUSBAND. "Difficulties which were so far from reasonable, that I was compelled to exert my authority as a husband, in order to induce you no longer to give to your son a milk which made him ill.   Your obstinacy almost cost us your own life and our child's."

THE MOTHER. "That is true."

X. "Your maternal tenderness, madam, was therefore in fault, since, but for your husband, you would have compromised the existence, or at least the health of your child, and all this for

* Nouveau Monde Industriel ; 2d edition, p. 204.

the sake of obeying the moralist Rousseau! Confess, madam, that in this instance your reason advised you badly."

THE MOTHER. "I acknowledged it afterwards; but no matter, the suffering I experienced when I was obliged to give up nursing my child, has proved to me that nursing is to all mothers a duty imposed by nature. Look, Sir, you who take all your examples from nature, look at the animals; do not all the females suckle their little ones? It is nature, it is God, who so wills it."

THE HUSBAND. "Upon this point, certainly, I should be entirely of my wife's opinion. Not only does nature give to the females the organs necessary to enable them to suckle their little ones, but she moreover sends to them, during the time the suckling must last, an increase of intelligence and of maternal tenderness. The will of nature is no less manifest as regards woman; for the secretion of the milk begins in the mother at the period of parturition. At the moment when the child needs nursing, the bosom of the mother is filled with a very light milk, with the milk which is fitted for a newly born child."

THE MOTHER. "That is evident, and I really do not conceive how any one can for a moment doubt the manifest will of nature"—

X. "Excuse me, madam, we are going a little too fast. There is truth in what you say; but your argument is incomplete; allow me to prove it to you.

"In many respects man resembles the animals. Therefore, we see him subject to the greater part of the laws which nature has imposed upon the latter. Still, in their application to man, those laws must undergo some modifications; you must clearly understand, in fact, that man, being a creature superior to the animal kingdom, and endowed with a number of faculties which have been refused to animals, God cannot have willed to subject him in every respect to the same régime as creatures of an inferior order."

THE HUSBAND. "Yes, I understand, and I admit that."

X. "Well! then, why should you not admit that, with respect to suckling, there is for man *something better to do than to follow the example given by animals?* Is not the life of our children in their early years, surrounded by many more guarantees than is that of the young of animals ?   If the latter are deprived of their mother, deserted by the only being whom nature has commis- sioned to watch over them, they are lost, they die of hunger. How different is it with the child of man !   In case of the loss of the mother, even of the father and other relatives, does not the young child, whom misfortune has made an orphan, find twenty persons instead of one, disposed to intervene in order to find for him a mother by adoption ?   and do not twenty women, who are moved to compassion at the sight of the poor little one, dispute among themselves for the honor of giving him a portion of the milk which each had intended for her own child ?   For the young of animals, the foresight of nature is *simple*, while for the chil- dren of the king of creation, it is *composite*.

"From another point of view—is it not recognised by physi- cians that a lymphatic woman, whose husband is likewise lymphatic, would act wisely in refraining from nursing her child, and in endeavoring to give to him a nurse of a sanguine temperament ?   Is it not recognised that, by means of precau- tions of this nature, parents might remedy a number of infirmi- ties or vices, which otherwise would become hereditary ?   Now, only the intelligence of man can combine these precautions, and upon this point it is not to the animals that we ought, and that we can go for lessons."

THE MOTHER. "Doubtless there must be a difference between man's style of acting, and that of the animals ; man being a *reasoning animal*—

X. "You have said it, madam, Man is a *reasoning animal*. But you must then allow us to be right when we blame that *rea- soning animal* for giving as a principle of moral philosophy, as a duty, a prescription which is in no sense based upon reason.

"THE FIRST DUTY of a mother is to *do that which is most for the advantage of her child*.   Now, in order to know if a particular mode of nursing be more or less suitable for such or such a child, we must consult reason and science, and act according to their decisions.   After this I shall agree with you that, in the greater number of cases, the mother will be found to be the most proper nurse for her child ; and as the accomplishment of this function of nurse is, and probably always will be, a great delight to mothers, I do not doubt that, in the phalansterian régime, the greater portion of them will nurse their children."

THE MOTHER. "Very well, sir, and now I agree with you."

X. "And you give up Rousseau?"

THE MOTHER. "Yes, I give up Rousseau."

X. "Poor Jean Jacques! If you were still alive, you who were so intelligent, how, on reading Fourier, you would blush at having written Emile!—

"But our digression upon nursing has made us lose sight of the principal subject of our conversation. We were speaking of public education, of its insufficiency, of its falsity. Do you wish to know its result? Take a young man as he leaves college; no one can be more artificial, he does everything awkwardly; he knows it, and this knowledge makes him more timid and more awkward still. And then try to question him: he is entirely ignorant of things which a child eight years old will know in Harmony; thus he becomes wearisome, in consequence of his asking about everything, being astonished at everything, and passing continually from one question to another, without even waiting for the answer, in such a hurry is he to have a solution upon other points! How many, who have just successfully passed an examination for their degree, are completely astonished when informed that by means of the triangles, respecting which they shortly before were questioned, a plan can be drawn, and the contents of a piece of land obtained! Why is this? I have told you, and it cannot be repeated too often; it is because science is presented to them in a manner so abstract, so repellent, so far removed from the application they must one day make of it, that they cannot perceive either the cause or the end of their studies. Thus they know almost nothing, and the little that they do know, they are hardly conscious of; therefore what happens?—

"A thing happens that every one has observed. It happens, often, that those who have shone most upon the benches of the school, are those who are least remarked in after life, while we see a great number of those whom the college had rejected, or left upon the lowest seats, distinguish themselves in the world. People are astonished, they complain at this result; and yet it is very simple. At college, they always endeavor to stimulate the same faculties in all children; even among those faculties they regard only the passive or neuter ones, memory first and then comparison—the whole confined in the circle of literary studies. From this it results, that a child moderately endowed and therefore malleable, makes great progress, so long as memory only is exercised in him, and still makes progress so long as only the passive parts of his intellect are brought into play. The strongly tempered natures, on the contrary, those in whom the active springs, such as imagination, invention, are very tense, very powerful, cannot accommodate themselves to such a régime. These natures revolt against a rule which cannot be fitted for them; far from being distinguished in the first phases of education, they go through them in the midst of punishments and cares, and for this very reason do not place themselves in a condition to succeed in the second phase, where they would have found more chances of success.

"Out of college, it is entirely different. Between the college and the world no bond has been formed, or more properly, an abyss has been dug. In the world, the active, creative faculties are the most precious. These faculties, having received no education, are in fact compelled to develop themselves, and then the individual, however well endowed he may be, incurs the most serious dangers. Either he is developed subversively, in consequence of the hindrances he meets upon his route, and you condemn him by saying, 'He is a miserable fellow, naturally perverse, with whom no one could ever do anything;' or else he is developed in a direction useful to his kind and to himself, and then how often you cry out: 'That's astonishing! he was the poorest scholar! and now you see what brilliant talents he has!' Those of his colleagues who had crushed him under the weight of their college triumphs, refuse to acknowledge his superiority until they are themselves crushed by it. What does this prove?— The opposition of our present education to nature, or rather the want, or what is still worse, the radical falseness of our methods of education.

"Poor young people! poor children! Is it their fault if we do not know how to discern their instincts, to develop their aptitudes? if we do not know how to bring to light their vocations;

and if, passing them under the same level we have foolishly wished to extend over society, we adopt a uniform rule for such different natures? Have we a good reason to make them afterwards pay by inflictions for the evil results of which our ignorance alone is the cause?

"If any one ought to be punished, whipped, is it not those schoolmasters who, conducting studies contrary to common sense, make us lose our best years in being wearied, vexed, in being falsified, corrupted by idleness, disgusts of every species? Why do they not follow the method of our nurses? Excellent teachers are our nurses! They teach us to talk without our perceiving it; and how? by taking advantage of our wants, of our instincts, of our desire to articulate sounds. If, instead of presenting science in a shape which renders it inaccessible to the intelligence of those poor children, our learned teachers would have the goodness to recollect a little of the lessons of their nurses (who, by the way, knew nothing of Greek and Latin); if, I say, they would try this natural method, the only one which is applicable to young children, in a word, if they would endeavor to make useful, to flatter their industrial manias; if they would provide them with tools fitted for their size, in *miniature* workshops, and if they knew how to establish among them common interests, corporative ties, a hierarchy, such as Nature wishes to establish among all the members of the human race, we should soon see the disorders, the idleness, the destructive habits of which we complain so much, disappear and be replaced by habits of order, of labor, of economy; we should see these dear children become earnest for useful, productive things, we should see them learn while they amuse themselves.

"How incredible it is! In all ages children have been amused with perfectly useless playthings, every day we invent new toys to employ their turbulent activity, and no one has yet thought of making their amusements serve for the development of their vocations; no one has yet thought of systematically giving to them useful playthings, *miniature tools*, which would amuse them, which would interest them much more than the trifles with which we now surround them!"

THE HUSBAND. "I think I can guess what you demand for children; you would wish them all to have a mechanical education."

X. "Yes, doubtless, a mechanical education; but here again we must have an understanding. The following is what will take place among us:

"For quite small children, education is entirely practical; afterwards some explanations will be united with the practice (children like explanations very much, they are greedy for them). The most intelligent will understand at once; others will require several repetitions; some will not understand at all, from which it must not be concluded that these last are entirely devoid of intelligence, but that their intelligence wishes to be exercised on other subjects.

"Therefore, we should never scold children: poor little ones! be sure that when they do not understand, the fault is not in them.

"When I speak of explanations to be given to young children, you feel plainly, madam, that I do not mean difficult theories; these will come later; they will come when the children ask for them, when they begin to feel the need of them. Those whom the difficulties of science do not repel, those whom they even *attract*, are the only ones to whom these difficulties should be explained. We do not compel any child to receive such or such a lesson, for we are fully persuaded that those whom Nature has destined to become savans will feel irresistibly drawn towards science, from the moment when we shall have simply known how to put them in contact with it. As to those whom science repels, those who, as is commonly said, do not bite at the theory, we leave them very quiet: another destiny calls them elsewhere. In all things, the will of Nature, the order of God, should be respected. Do you not think, madam, that we are right in acting thus?"

THE MOTHER. "Everything you say, sir, appears to me very just; we always repent having wished to force a child to do anything that did not please him. In this respect I differ in opinion from many parents of my acquaintance, who are delighted when they have succeeded in making their child do their will: they are proud of the least victory obtained over nature ; it would seem that they made a merit of overcoming the difficulty. The tears of the child do not stop them ; they pursue the plan of studies they have adopted with a perseverance which I myself call cruelty ; and after much trouble on their part and much ennui and disgust on that of the child, they attain only a very moderate result."

X. "Oh! madam, how pleased I am to find that such are your feelings! You will understand, you will love Fourier's Theory.

"Look at the superiority of our system over that in present use! With us a professor has for pupils only those children who really *wish* to receive his lessons. What pleasure he therefore has, and what success! all his young audience are animated with the desire of learning, and give the most earnest attention to his words ; the greatest silence prevails in the class ; the time of the lesson slips away before the pupils perceive it ; for them it is always too short : I should like to have you see them follow the professor into the court-yard and overwhelm him with fresh questions. But he, in order to keep them earnest, in order that they may still be desirous of the next lesson, refuses to answer them, he sends them off to other labors—that is, to other plays—"

THE HUSBAND. "Which method of teaching will you choose? Will you adopt mutual or simultaneous instruction ?"

THE MOTHER. "As to myself, it seems to me that mutual instruction is preferable : I have seen really astonishing things in the mutual schools. It seems to me that nothing could be better."

X. "We are not exclusive in the matter of methods ; you may be sure that there will be more than two methods in the Phalanstery ; one for one thing, another for another ; and besides, such a method will be suitable for some pupils, which will not be suitable for others—In fine, we shall do that which will be most appropriate in each particular case.

"Mutual instruction is based on two incontestable natural facts : 1st. The child who is older or more intelligent than his comrades is always delighted to show his superiority over them, and asks nothing better than to become their professor, their *monitor ;* 2d. The younger are always inclined to imitate their elder comrades, and even to obey their orders with the greatest docility (this is what Fourier calls the *progressive attraction from the weak to the strong*). These two natural inclinations are turned to use in mutual instruction, and in part explain the beautiful results which you have seen, madam. What is most astonishing in a numerous mutual school, is the great facility with which children, naturally so active and so noisy, are kept in the most perfect order and even in the most complete silence during the time of the lessons. This fact excites the admiration of those who witness it, they give credit for it to the master, who, I assure you, is frequently very innocent in the matter."

THE MOTHER. "How do you explain that ?"

X. "In the following manner, madam. Among children as well as among men, the *mass* exercises a very great influence over the *individual*. Whatever the *mass* has adopted, whatever becomes the *tone* in a great assemblage, is accepted and adopted by each of the individuals ; no one of them would dare to contradict the opinion of the *mass*—so long, be it understood, as he forms a part of that *mass*. If this natural inclination of the individual did not exist, *order* could not subsist without *constraint*. But it would be wrong to conclude from this remark, that it is impossible to realize *order* while leaving to the *individual* an entire *liberty of action*. This, on the contrary, is *very possible*, owing to the deference which every individual *naturally* has for the *mass*."

THE HUSBAND. " This deference of the individual for the mass, my dear friend, does not appear to me a very solid basis, a sufficient guarantee for *order*. Children, especially, reason so little, are so active and so turbulent ! If the masters did not hold them in a little severely, I should fear greatly that their deference for the *mass* would not be enough to keep them long in order—and then how will you manage to make that *mass* will order, especially if it is a *mass* of little devils ?"

X. "You may be easy. God, who wills *order*, has foreseen all necessities, and here, with his almighty power, has made use of a general and infallible method ; he has given to the great majority of men a *taste*, an *attraction*, for regular, measured, cadenced motions, for those beautiful movements of a whole, which masses alone can execute.   As soon as it is proposed to masses to accomplish these regular movements, the great majority accept with joy, with enthusiasm ; the greatest devils are calmed, and take their places in the ranks of the mass."

" What is it that I hear ?" said the mother with an involuntary thrill.

X. " That which you hear, madam ?—eh ! zounds ! it is my proof coming most apropos."

THE MOTHER. " How ? what proof?"

X. " The proof of the power of the *measured mode* upon the great majority of men.   What you hear is nothing else than a company of soldiers coming this way with a drum."

" Soldiers ! soldiers !" said little Mary, rushing to the balcony. " How lucky ! here's a company !"

" Mamma ! my dear good little mamma," cried the brother, coming hurriedly out of the study, " do let me see the soldiers go by. I entreat you, mamma ! you shall see how well I will learn my fables afterwards."

All of us, great and small, went and installed ourselves upon the balcony.

" Well, madam," said X., when the troop had passed, " is it not true that these regular movements have an attractive, an irresistible power ?   And you will notice that the crowd which accompanies the music and surrounds it on every side, is attracted there, not by a wish to look at the uniforms, but by the desire to join in the cadenced movement of the tune, and to march in step."

THE MOTHER. " It is so, doubtless, Sir, but any one could have remarked that."

X. " Yes, madam, any one ;. but Fourier alone has recognised that this is a NATURAL LAW, a constant one ; Fourier alone has found the means to make an application of it, an application useful to the facts of social life, and especially to those of education.

" But this application exists already, and if I did not fear to abuse your obligingness, I would read to you the recital of a visit made by one of our friends, some years since, to one of the halls of asylum at Paris."

THE MOTHER. " How so, Sir ?—It is yourself who are obliging, and we request you to continue."

X. " Since you give me permission, madam, I will read our friend's delightful narration.

" ' The Halls of Asylum are already numerous in Paris, where the first was founded in 1828. Visit a Hall of Asylum, if you are not yet acquainted with those good and pious establishments ; there is no sight in Paris which will give you a better or a sweeter emotion. The object of the Hall of Asylum is to receive the children of the surrounding quarter during the day. The establishment is composed of a court-yard planted with trees and provided with a spacious shed. In fine weather the children play in the yard, in the sun ; they gather under the shed when it rains. From seven in the morning, the mothers or the large sisters bring the children to the Asylum, where they remain until seven in the evening ; they are received from the age of twenty-two months up to six years.

" ' Now, you will see in the court three hundred little children, full of gaiety and activity, playing, leaping, jumping rope, and rolling upon the sand in the sun—and for these three hundred children one single superintendent !—I have seen in the Hall of Asylum of the Rue Saint Hippolyte, a little miniature garden dazzling with flowers, and in the middle of the flowers a dwarf cherry-tree, no higher than the children of three or four years old, who were playing close beside it ; that cherry-tree was covered with beautiful red cherries, which each of the children could have gathered by simply stretching out a hand. Well ! not one of those pretty cherries was touched, all those pretty flowers were respected ! and note, if you please, that these little children are very free, for frequently the director is out of sight, and remains whole half-hours without showing himself. Better still ! when new children arrive at the Asylum, as soon as they approach the little garden, it is the others who inform them that it is *not to be touched*, and no one does touch it. There has never been a scolding to give, a punishment to inflict on this account ; yet the temptation is great. It is the influence of the tone which prevails there, the influence of the unitary tone.

" ' But what follows is pretty. When all these little children are amusing themselves in their court, where they amuse themselves so much, that *at least half of them*, as the good director told us, *would forget to eat, and leave their little baskets full of food without touching them, if he did not take care;* when they are amusing themselves so much, I said, the master gives a whistle. At this whistle, little girls and little boys suddenly quit their play, and come to place themselves in file, each in his rank: three hundred children, and among them twenty-two months' old babies! and there is perfect silence! "Attention, my children!" says the master; and at the second whistle, all cross their hands behind their backs. At the third whistle, the master beating time with a wooden staff, the two regiments of little girls and little boys begin to march, marking the step and singing to the air of Marlborough:

> " ' Nous nous mettons en marche,
>   Mironton, ton, ton, mirontaine;
>   Nous nous mettons en marche,
>   Pour aller travailler;
>   Car il faut s'occuper
>   Pour ne pas s'ennuyer,
>   Pour ne pas s'ennuyer.'

" ' And there they are marching in measure in two files, always singing in measure, and singing to one air at first, then to another, then to a third, all the movements which they make, all the evolutions which they execute while going in good order, to take their accustomed places upon the benches of the school. The master gives a whistle, everything stops, march and song. There is a perfect silence, you could hear the buzzing of a fly. When the measure is resumed, the march and song are resumed—It is wonderful.

" ' I will not describe the series of little exercises of reading, of numeration, of movements, which they are made to execute during the two hours that the session lasts, and which they do execute, sometimes singing, sometimes not singing, but always regularly, always simultaneously, always *in measure.* This would take too long. Go and see the Hall of Asylum in the Rue Saint Hippolyte; it is the most interesting because it is the most numerous. Go and see it, and you will not regret your trouble, and you will understand what can be accomplished, on such young masses, with singing, with a regular step, with a cadenced movement, with the employment, though so weak and so confused, of the *measured mode.*

" ' Close to the court and the hall of the very little ones, are the court and the halls of the mutual schools of the larger children. Three hundred boys in the mutual school of the boys,

3

three hundred girls in the mutual school of the girls, learn to read, to write, to draw, are taught arithmetic, geometry, and the musical scale, under the direction of a single master and a single mistress.   Here then, in consequence of imitation, in consequence of mutualism, in consequence of the progressive ascending attraction, but especially in consequence of a still greatly restricted employment of the measured mode, we see six hundred children and more, kept, governed, taught, under the direction of three grown persons.

"'I say six hundred and more, for there have sometimes been as many as eleven hundred children present at the establishment in the Rue Saint Hippolyte.   Really, we are not permitted to close our eyes upon such revelations.   Only figure to yourself these eleven hundred children passing the day, each isolatedly in their families, and calculate the follies they will commit ; the trouble and anxiety they will cost their parents ; the cries they will utter, the tears they will shed !   Thus the master of the Hall of Asylum will tell you, what I knew very well beforehand : IT IS MUCH EASIER TO TAKE CARE OF AND TO BRING UP THREE OR FOUR HUNDRED, THAN TO TAKE CARE OF AND TO BRING UP THREE OR FOUR.'"*

THE MOTHER. "Oh ! it is strikingly true."

THE HUSBAND. "Yes, certainly ! it is entirely conclusive ; and I now understand the power of the *mass* over the *individual*."

X. "You see from this how useful mutual instruction may be. But for many things, I myself am of opinion that the lesson should be given by a professor ; in other terms, that simultaneous teaching should be adopted, combining it sometimes with mutual instruction."

THE MOTHER. "You spoke just now of the *progressive attraction of the weak to the strong :* what does that mean ?   In spite of the explanations you have given on this subject, there still remains some obscurity in my mind."

X. "If you attentively examine an assemblage of children, you will there see that very naturally THE STRONG *attract* THE WEAK, that is, the child of five *always* seeks to imitate the example given to him by the child of six ; he of six the example which the child of seven gives him, and so on in succession, following the progression of ages.   This tendency to imitation is less decided from the child of five years old to one of ten, the distance is too great ;

* *Destinée Sociale*, by V. Considerant, vol. III. *Education.*

and this is why a family education is so little fitted for the development of vocations; because the child brought up at home often wants the examples and the stimulants which he very naturally finds among children of his own age."

THE MOTHER. "Thank you, sir, for your explanation; now I understand."

X. "Ah! madam, why have you not time to study, in the writings of our Master, all that relates to education! With what love has Fourier treated this subject! With what truly paternal solicitude has he foreseen and calculated all that is necessary to those little beings who are so dear to us! If you only knew, madam, how happy mothers will be at the Phalanstery! how much they will enjoy the good condition and the progress of their children! what touching accords, what strong and sincere friendships will be formed between the mothers and the bonnes or adoptive nurses! what delicious exchanges of gratitude and sympathy will be produced by that admirable institution of empassioned *corporative Maternity!* If you knew all this, how anxious you would be to see the erection of the first Phalanstery."

"You, madam, who are afflicted at finding in your children instincts for dirt, or inclinations for luxury, would then recognise with joy, how useful, when they are well employed, are all the tastes of little children, all their defects (as they are called), such as the inclination for dirt, the taste for kitchen work, the love of sweet things, gluttony in fine, gluttony, that taste so general in children, that precious tendency which is very wrongly repressed in our day, and which causes those poor little ones to shed so many tears, which costs them so many vexations! No! It is not without reason that Nature has caused children to be born with these tastes, with these inclinations! Instead of being repressed, these tastes wish to be turned to use, these inclinations wish to be developed, refined; and Fourier demonstrates this victoriously by the charming details which he gives of the relations and the labors of the Tribes of childhood. There is, in fact, nothing more delightful than his conception of the LITTLE HORDES and the LITTLE BANDS, two infantile corporations arriving, one at the *beautiful* by the route of the *good*, the other at the *good* by the route of the *beautiful;* this presiding over the maintenance of *social charm*, that having for its object the maintenance of *social unity*, and on this account surnamed MILITIA OF UNITY, a name to which it has every right from its devotedness and its civic virtues."

THE MOTHER. " Please explain that to us also, sir."

X. "Oh! madam, it would be necessary to enter into much too extensive details. Let it be enough for you to know that your son, who takes delight, you say, in dirt, and who, consequently, would be very properly classed in the category of little black-guards, your son would perhaps have a very honorable and a very lucrative rank in the body of the LITTLE HORDES. As to your little Mary, she would perhaps be a chief of series in the corporation of the LITTLE BANDS. But in order to explain to you this admirable machinery, it would be necessary to go to the bottom of this inexhaustible subject ; it would be necessary to place before your eyes all the resources of the societary order ; it would be necessary to show to you how children, so rebellious with our present methods, so restive under the gloomy and solitary exercises to which we condemn them, are empassioned in the measured exercises of serial education ; and, besides, you could satisfy yourself of all this by studying the instincts of your children, at the same time that you study social science."

THE MOTHER. " Oh! sir, how can you expect a woman to undertake such difficult matters ?"

X. " Be undeceived, madam; the social science, far from being encompassed by difficulties, as you might believe, presents, on the contrary, the most attractive details. As it indicates the *causes* and the *ends* of things, it has not that character of dryness and obscurity with which we reproach other sciences. And why do we find so many difficulties in studying the sciences in general ? Precisely because we are not taught either the *causes* or the *ends* of things ; because frequently we are not even presented with an analysis, but only with a simple announcement which speaks neither to the heart nor to the imagination. For example, if we were taught natural history, botany, chemistry, in such a manner as to show us their relation with the various natural and social phenomena, their analogy with our passions ; all these sciences, far from being repulsive, as they now are, would become speaking, animated pictures; and not only should we learn by heart the most minute details, but we should moreover make much less effort to furnish our memory with a quantity of notions which it cannot now retain."

THE MOTHER. "But, sir, in order to teach natural history, geography and the other sciences as you would wish, it would first be necessary to know them in that manner, it would require an immense learning."

X. "Yes, madam; whence I conclude that the present education of our colleges and family education are both bad and incomplete, because they are far from being able to provide the necessary elements, elements which the social science alone can furnish, which the societary order alone can apply. You see, madam, all things are bound, are chained together, the evil as well as the good, and it is because we alone know how to solve the other social problems, that we alone know how to solve the important problem of education. Moreover, the study of UNIVERSAL ANALOGY, explaining the causes and ends of creation, presents so many charms, so many attractions, especially to ladies, that I ask your permission to communicate to you hereafter a little work on this subject.

"Analogy is really a romantic, an enchanting science. By it—a thing which would appear impossible—the love of the marvellous, so common among men, so attractive to all ages, agrees always with reason.

"Certainly, madam, if you were made to see why such a flower has such a conformation, why such a color; if you were made acquainted with the symbolical relation which exists between such a passion, such a character, such individual and social manners, and the form, size, color, the peculiar odor, the habits of such a plant, such a flower, or such an animal; if, in fine, you had explained to you Figaro's question: *Why these things and not others?* (a question which children never fail to ask), this word, *Science*, applied to the different notions of natural objects of all orders, far from frightening, would strongly attract you."

THE MOTHER. "Yes, sir, I accept that fully."

X. "Well! if grown persons perceive how contrary to common sense are our methods of education, why should they be astonished that children profit so little by those methods? Far from knowing how to direct them, they do not even know how to let them learn by themselves, they know only how to repress their natural inclinations, while those inclinations ought to be developed."

THE MOTHER. "I agree with you, and all that is very well so long as you suppose that children display only suitable inclinations."

X. "What do you call suitable inclinations?"

THE MOTHER. "I mean inclinations which suit the parents, the family."

X. "Well! Did I not say, just now, that in civilization, parents have the mania (a fatal one) of wishing to find reproduced in their children, their own tastes, their own inclinations, or at least an aptitude for the career to which they destine them? And when Nature balks this desire (which is almost always the case), the parents do not consider themselves overcome; no! they compress the natural tastes of their children in order to inculcate factitious ones. This is contrary to common sense, and involves a real danger to individuals as well as to society. And it is thus, by falsifying the character and vocations of children, that are produced bad sons, bad husbands, bad fathers, bad citizens."

THE MOTHER. "But yet, if my son or my daughter had vulgar tastes, low tastes—"

X. "In our day, doubtless, that would be vexatious to you, madam, very vexatious to your family who would have to blush for them; but, in the Phalanstery, no such thing is known as a low taste. In truth, by the single fact of the organization of labor, every function is ennobled, there is no longer any mean trade, any despised work, and your son could yield to all his inclinations without occasioning to you the slightest dishonor. Now, see the immense advantage which results from this:

" 'Such a child,' " says Fourier,[*] " " 'although the son of a prince, testifies from three years old a taste for the trade of a cobbler, and wishes to frequent the hall of the cobblers, *who are as polished in Association as any other persons.* If he is prevented, if his cobbling mania is repressed, under the pretext that it is not of the philosophical standard, he will become irritated against his other

---

[*] Nouveau Monde Industriel, 2d edition, p. 188.

functions, will acquire no taste for the labors and studies to which it is considered desirable to attract him; but if he is allowed to commence by the point to which Attraction leads him, he will soon be tempted to take cognisance of shoemaking, of tannery, then of chemistry with reference to the various preparations of leather, then of agronomy with reference to the qualities which the skins of animals may acquire by such or such a system of education and régime, such or such a kind of pasturage.

"'By degrees he will be initiated into all the industries in consequence of a first emulation in *cobbling*; the point by which he shall have commenced will be of very little consequence, provided he attains in the course of his youth general knowledges upon all the branches of industry practised in his Phalanx, and provided he conceives an affection for all the Series which shall have initiated him into them.

"'This instruction cannot be acquired in civilization where nothing is connected. The savans tell us that the sciences form a chain, each link of which is fastened to the whole and leads from one to the other; but they forget that our parcelled relations sow discord among all classes of industry, which renders each indifferent to the labors of another, while in a Phalanx each is interested in all the series, in consequence of intrigues with some of their members, in gastronomy, the opera, agriculture, &c. The bond of the sciences is, therefore, not sufficient to attract to studies; it is necessary to unite with it the bond of functions, of individuals, of rival intrigues, a thing which is impracticable in civilization.'"

THE HUSBAND. "Can you give us an instance of the application of this law to the facts of social and industrial life?"

X. "Let us defer this question until another day, if you please; but since we have spoken of Analogy, allow me to cite to you some pictures of the master. They have a reference to children. This is a temptation which I exercise upon you, madam; you must beware—Speaking of the MIGNONETTE:

"'The Mignonette,'" says Fourier, "'represents the industrious children of the societary order. Its flower has no visible petals; it is composed only of the productive parts, stamens and pistil, from allegory to the children of Harmony, incessantly busied in productive functions and finding pleasure only in the useful labors which they execute in a number of passional series; by analogy, the mignonette suppresses the petals, emblems of unproductive pleasure. A very sweet perfume escapes from this little flower, in symbol of the charm excited by children passionately addicted to useful industry. Nature gives to the stamens the capucine color, a mixture of red and orange (color of enthusiasm and ambition), in symbol of the industrial lever of the harmonian children, which is enthusiasm sustained by ambition.

" ' Beneath the flowers comes a long row of little sacks partially filled and open; this is the emblem of all the little treasures amassed by the harmonian child in his youth—when he expends but little, and usually accumulates some fifty small sums saved from the dividends obtained in the different series he has frequented. Their aggregate composes a little fortune which is given to the child when he is fifteen. There is but little seed in the capsules, because the child cannot earn very large dividends in his series. Nature has left the sacks open, although turned downwards; this shows a double want of prudential precautions, from analogy to the impossibility of deceiving and defrauding a harmonian child, although he disdains every precaution against craft and theft.

" ' This picture cannot be applied to the habits of civilized children. From this it may be understood that it is impossible to study vegetable and animal analogies so long as men are ignorant of the machinery of the Periods of Harmony, to which refer many of the plants, such as the jasmine, violet, pansy, mignonette, serpentine, cacao, the analogy of which does not exist in the manners and customs of civilization.

" ' But from the moment when one is acquainted with the customs of the eight social Periods, he can find their portraits in the vast museum of the four kingdoms where the effects of our Passions are hieroglyphically depicted. Until then naturalists can only observe EFFECTS, without knowing the CAUSES which have decided God in his distributive operations. If they are asked why the lily is endowed with a pollen which perfidiously soils the face of man; why the pink ruptures its calyx irregularly, they are compelled to take refuge in the *profound profundities of the decrees, and the thick thickness of the veils of brass.* Which means in vulgar language, that they know nothing of the calculation of CAUSES; that their studies are limited to the simple modes or classification of EFFECTS.

" ' If we are ignorant of the causes which have presided over each detail of creation, we are every moment tempted to criticize Nature and its wise Author, whose faithful pencil we should admire, if we knew how to determine, by analogy, the meaning of their pictures. On seeing a mignonette, each one cries: What a pity that so sweetly perfumed a little flower is not somewhat more ornamented, that it has not brilliant petals! And then this medley of capsules almost without seed—this is a useless superfluity! thus expresses itself civilized or *simple* reason, which knows only effects and not causes. We have seen above that the picture would not be a true one, if God had made a single one of these corrections; the mignonette would not depict the industrial customs of children in the eighth Period; and the lily which did not besmear civilized noses, would not be the exact interpreter of the dangers incurred by him who wishes to practise truth and uprightness in civilization.'"

THE MOTHER. "That is a charming picture; I regret only the last feature."

X. "How so?"

THE MOTHER. "Yes, I confess to you that I love the lily a great deal; it is so pure, so simple, so graceful a flower, that instead of looking upon it as opposed to truth and uprightness, it seems to me—ah! you are smiling, it is not well—yes? eh! well, yes, I confess it, I am led, by instinct, to consider the lily as an emblem of innocence."

X. "Do you wish, madam, to know the whole of Fourier's thought respecting this flower?"

THE MOTHER. "Ah! let us see."

X. "'The stalk of the lily is straight and firm like the course of the truthful man. It is distinguished by a frame of graceful little leaves: thus the honorable and truthful man shines by the traces of esteem which he leaves in all his industrial or administrative functions (leaf and labor are synonymous).

"'The corolla, like that of the tulip, is a triangle without calyx, from analogy to the truthful man (lily), and the just man (tulip). Their conduct is not enveloped in any mystery, and is uncovered: thus the bulbous root of the lily is half-opened in every part in detached blades, and allows the interior to be seen, from analogy to the course of the loyal man, whose principles, and the depth of whose heart are open to inspection.

"'This flower, the emblem of purity and uprightness, has two strange qualities: it is *perfidious* and *banished*.

"'1st, *perfidious*, in that it besmears with a yellowish powder him who approaches it, attracted by its perfume. This stain, which excites laughter, represents the fate of those who make a familiar use of truth.

"'Let a man who is docile to the lessons of philosophers, and resolved to practise *august truth, which is,* they say, *the best friend of mankind,* go into a saloon and tell the frank and honest truth about the ways and actions of those present, about the knaveries of the business men, and the intrigues of the ladies, he will be spit upon, treated as a philosophical ostrogoth, a clown inadmissible to good society. Every one, by an invitation to leave the room, will prove to him that *august truth is by no manner of means the best friend of mankind*, and can only lead to disgrace all who wish to practise it.

" ' Nature has written this lesson for us in the pollen with which she has endowed the stamens of the lily. It seems that she has intended to say to the man attracted by this flower : *distrust truth, do not rub yourself against it*. This is the object of the besmearing which she occasions upon those imprudent noses which unguardedly rub against the flower of the lily, and make themselves a moment afterwards pointed at by children, as a man makes himself pointed at by fathers, when he ventures to tell them the *august truth*.

" ' 2d, *Banished*. Truth is beautiful, if you will, but beautiful when seen at a distance, and such is the opinion of the world, since it cannot admit the flower of truth. No one would present a bouquet of lilies to a woman in good society ; no lilies are seen in the saloon of a Crœsus. Beautiful as this flower is, neither its form, its perfume, nor its brilliancy are suitable to the class of sybarites. They like the lily only at a distance, as they do truth ; they banish it to the angles of the flower-garden. The flower, as a bouquet, is suitable only to persons who do not fear weighty truths. Thus we see the lily figure in the public fêtes, and at the doors of wine-shops, where truth prevails. It charms children who do not fear frank and honest truth. Finally, it is used to ornament the statues and portraits of saints on festival days ; and it is very right to place the symbol of truth between the hands of the inhabitants of heaven ; for if it be well received in the other world, it is by no means so here.' "

THE MOTHER. "Oh ! that is strikingly true ; it is perfect, and I am very happy that Fourier thus justifies my partiality for the lily. But that is not all, doubtless, and you must still have something in reserve."

X. " Yes, I have the red fruits."

THE MOTHER. " Ah ! let us see the red fruits."

X. made a sign to me, and continued his quotations.

" ' The CHERRY, an image of the tastes of childhood, is the first fruit of the fine season. It is, in the order of gatherings, what childhood is in the order of ages. Friendship governs in the first phase among children, and love in the second phase among adults; it is necessary, from analogy, that the fruits of friendship should be the first, and those of love in the second line. Hence it is that the red fruits, or those having the amicable title, are followed by those with stones, fruits of love to which succeed the pears, emblems of the ambition which governs in the third phase called virility; the march is closed by the apples, emblem of the family love which rules in the fourth phase, or old age.

"'The cherry, portrait of free, happy, and merry children, must excite in them the effects which it represents. Thus the appearance of a basket of cherries delights all the infantile tribe, for whom this fruit is very healthy. The cherry is a plaything which nature presents to the child; he forms of it garlands and ear-rings; he crowns himself with it, as Silenus is crowned with leafy vine-branches. The tree is analogous to the genius and labors of childhood; it is scantily provided with leaves; its branches vaguely distributed, give but little shade, offer no guarantee either against the rain or the sun: image of the weak resources of childhood, it is incomplete, insufficient to protect and shelter man.' "

THE MOTHER. "Bravo! That is good! very good!"

X. "Now for the strawberry:

"'The STRAWBERRY is the most precious of the red fruits; it depicts to us the child brought up in Harmony, in the industrial groups; a strawberry plant is a laborer that goes to work like our gardener, its running stalk plants a file of shoots in a straight line. It is right that the most precious of children, he who exercises combined industry, should have for an emblem the most delicate fruit of the series. The leaf is ternary, in allusion to the three choirs which direct education. The strawberry, like the peach, is willing to form an alliance with wine and sugar, emblems of the passions *friendship* and *unityism;* thus the societary labor is sustained by friendship and tends to unity.'

"Now do you wish some currants?"

THE MOTHER. "Oh! yes, some currants, I beg of you."

X. "I have several to offer to you.

"'CURRANTS represent civilizee children of various classes. The most remarkable is the *red cluster currant;* it is the emblem of children who are but little cultivated and are given up to good Nature. They have a biting and indiscreet frankness; are capable of going and repeating to a woman of pretence any unpleasant truth they may have heard you utter.

"'The fruit which depicts these little truth-tellers must have a very piquant flavor. It is graceful, because Truth is graceful in a child and amuses in spite of the indiscretion. Such a character is not without utility; it notices oddities—*castigat ridendo*. Thus the fruit of the red currant is purgative and healthy. The plant is similar in leaves and clusters to the VINE, emblem of composite friendship; thus these free, loquacious, indiscreet children, are the most addicted to simple friendship. This kind of currant is a common fruit and of medium value, like the class of children which it represents; uncooked, it figures on few tables; it is not much used except in alliance with sugar and the labor of the confectioner; so children who are too free and unpolished, only become of value by accommodating themselves to the manners of the most elevated class.

" ' *The thorny currant with isolated fruit* depicts the restrained child, deprived of pleasures, harassed with moral philosophy and brought up in isolated studies. His emblem gives only a fruit of a poor kind, *pale violet*, color of blasted friendship, the development of which is thwarted in this scholar, by isolating him from his comrades. These children bloated with precepts and premature studies, generally become very ordinary individuals. Thus the hieroglyphic fruit, in spite of its beautiful appearance, is a product of but little value, swollen with insipid juices and superfluous seeds, like the children who are overloaded with badly digested teaching. This currant bush is thorny, in sign of the discomfort of the unfortunate children it depicts.

" ' *The black currant*, called *cassis*, represents poor and rude children; thus its black fruit, emblematic of poverty, has a bitter and disagreeable taste, from analogy to those children of the people who have the defect of bad language, bad manners, and often bad principles. They can be made endurable only by refining them in contact with the rich and polished class; so the cassis becomes eatable only by an alliance with brandy and sugar.' "

THE MOTHER. " What finesse! what observation! Have you not other fruits ?"

X. " I could have many others; but I see that the temptation takes effect. I shall be careful not to prolong an already too much extended visit, and I moreover wish that you may have something to ask of me the next time I come."

And we said farewell to our hosts.

formed services less poorly paid, because more difficult; later still they did whatever was asked of them, Jacques for the sake of drink, Jane for a collar or a piece of lace. Every day they are ready to sell themselves to any one who shall offer money; and their children will be brought up to the same life.

Simon is cooper in a wine store: even in his apprenticeship he was convinced, from the example of his master, that the profit was in proportion to the differences of measure, to the various mixtures which are made, sometimes to the detriment of the excise, sometimes to the prejudice of the purchaser or the seller. Simon now sees in all this only a necessity of his trade. The principal feature of his moral education has been the habit of fraud.

Lawrence is a shop-keeper: it is so well known that business is merely the art of buying cheap and selling dear, that it is quite superfluous to say what must have been the moral education of Lawrence.

Alphonse is head clerk in a public office: having incessantly before his eyes the example of his superiors, he has not been able to avoid the influences of their proximity; he has acquired habits of display, of expense, his wife has wished to make a show, debts have come, and all their moral education must have been directed to the methods of eluding payment and of finding, *per fas aut nefas*, the means of sustaining their position.

Edward, born rich, is accustomed to command, to compel obedience, to want nothing. Taught by numerous masters, lectured by his teachers, Edward sees on one side, only obstacles to his pleasures, on the other, only the means of enjoyment: to remove the first, to taste the last, is the moral education of the rich. To him, dissipation, extravagances, are what coarseness is to Jacques, craft to Simon, cheatery to Lawrence, indelicacy to Alphonse.

All professions, all conditions in society, have thus a special tendency in moral education, which does not prevent there being, in each profession or condition, men of honor actuated by noble sentiments. Unhappily, the number is so small, that they can only be considered as confirmatory exceptions.

Generally, the paths to well-being, in the existing social order, are so rare, so precarious, so little conformable to the laws of honesty, of good faith, of justice; the elements of moral education are usually so mixed, so vitiated, that the frauds, the spoliations, the collusions which our eyes constantly witness, even if we are not ourselves the victims, should not occasion any surprise. * * * * *

JUST MUIRON.